*Warrior: Reversing Disability from Multiple Sclerosis through
Strength Training, A Couple's Personal Journey*

By
David A. Phillipy
Copyright © 2014

Table of Contents

Introduction
> Page 1

Chapter 1      An Unwelcome Guest
> Page 6

Chapter 2      What We Did
> Page 39

Chapter 3      What You May Do
> Page 84

Chapter 4      In Summary
> Page 107

Addendum
Page 110

Introduction

My wife Carol has had Multiple Sclerosis, (MS), for more than thirty-five years. Over the course of time the disease has taken its toll by creating disability in a variety of ways. Having said that, she is a warrior. This is a story of how she has fought the disease. It is a story of how we as a couple have fought the disease with me as her caregiver and strength trainer.

MS and Other Neurological Degenerative Disorders

Multiple Sclerosis means "multiple scars" which may appear on a MRI of the brain and spinal column. MS can affect virtually any area of the body and mind and varies considerably from one person to another. No two people experience MS and its symptoms exactly alike. While this work is about reversing disability caused by MS, it is worth noting that progressive resistance training, (PRT), has been useful in managing and reversing symptoms with other neurological diseases including post-polio syndrome, Parkinson's disease, and stroke.

In reference to PRT training with post-polio patients, James C. Agre, Md, PhD, explained, "...we conducted a 12-

week study of muscle-strengthening exercise in seven post-polio subjects. Subjects exercised four times per week for 12 weeks at home. Exercise intervals were interspersed with rest breaks. After the 12week program, the average increase in strength was 36%; also work capacity and endurance increased by 15% or more."[1]

With Parkinson's Disease, it was found, "Weight training twice a week may reduce the stiffness, slowness, and tremors often seen in people with Parkinson's disease, a new study shows. ... In the study, 48 people with Parkinson's disease participated in a weight-training program or another program aimed at improving flexibility, balance, and strength. Participants exercised for one hour twice a week for two years. They were aged 59, on average, and had had Parkinson's for about seven years.

---

[1] Agre, James C., MD, PhD, Woodruff, Wisconsin, "The Role of Activity," *Post-Polio Health,* Vol 15, No. 2, Spring 1999

Everyone saw benefits after six months, but these benefits lasted two years among those in the weight- training group."[2]

Similar results for PRT were found with stroke patients. "We have shown for the first time in a direct comparison study that high-intensity PRT, but not cycling or sham exercise, can improve muscle strength, peak power, and muscle endurance in both affected and unaffected lower limbs after chronic stroke by a significant and clinically meaningful amount. Although strength gains plateaued earlier than anticipated, adherence to the

---

[2] Mann, Denise, WebMD Health News, "Weight Training Improves Parkinson's Symptoms, Twice-Weekly Resistance Training Sessions Can Improve Tremors, Slowness, and Rigidity," Parkinson's Disease Health Center, WebMD, Feb. 16, 2012, ©2012, WebMD, LLC. All rights reserved.

intended continuous high-intensity progressive overload protocol was largely achieved…."[3]

"I was pushed hard, so that I was falling, but the Lord helped me. *The Lord is my strength* and my song; he has become my salvation." Psalms 118: 13-14

In our experience with MS, we have found that an aggressive regimen of strength training, (ST), through a combination of resistance machines and free weights has reversed Carol's disability on multiple matrices. The terms ST, PRT and resistance training, (RT) may be used interchangeably. Having said that, it is advisable to consult a physician before engaging in an exercise program.

This book is written in the hope that those who read it may use it to either stop or reverse the disabling

---

[3] Lee, MJ, Kilbreath, SL, Singh, MF, Zeman, B, Davis, GM, "Effect of progressive resistance training on muscle performance after chronic stroke," *Medical Science Sports Exercise,* 2010, January; 42 (1), 23-34.

effects of MS in their lives or the life of someone they care for.

## Chapter 1: An Unwelcome Guest

MS sucks.

Carol calls her MS "an unwelcome guest." I call that unwelcome guest a "sociopath." This sociopath shows no remorse or empathy. That's the way sociopaths are. He steals multiple functions from his MS victims. He steals from body, mind and spirit. In his stealing he creates multiple stressors for the loved ones and caregivers of those with MS. The burglar has a long list of things which he steals. Areas affected by MS include but are not necessarily limited to loss of walking ability; fatigue; numbness and tingling in limbs; poor balance and coordination; loss of dexterity in hands and fingers;

changes in vision; dizziness and vertigo; problems in thinking; concentration and memory; mood changes including depression; muscle stiffness/spasticity; pain; loss of bladder and bowel control, and sexual dysfunction.

Sensitivity to heat is another frequent symptom. Excessive heat short-circuits the nerves leading to more susceptibility to falling and increasing fatigue. "In a study published in 2011, Swedish researchers found that more than 70 percent of all MS patients experience some degree of heat sensitivity."[4] Any of these symptoms by themselves or in combination may be disabling.

The sociopath steals sexual pleasure. Sexual dysfunction is often a difficult topic to talk about between patient and doctor and between patient and intimate

---

[4] "Multiple Sclerosis Patients Especially Sensitive to Heat," HealthlineNews, Copyright © 20052014 Healthline Networks, Inc.

partner. It is noted that, "Primary sexual dysfunction stems directly from MS-related changes in the brain and spinal cord that affect the sexual response or the ability to feel sexual pleasure. In both men and women, this can include a decrease or loss of sex drive, decreased or unpleasant genital sensations, and diminished capacity for orgasm. Men may experience difficulty achieving or maintaining an erection and a decrease in or loss of ejaculatory force or frequency. Women may experience decreased vaginal lubrication, loss of vaginal muscle tone and/or diminished clitoral engorgement."[5]

Secondary sexual dysfunction does not directly involve nerve pathways but nonetheless impair sexual pleasure. These symptoms may include bladder and bowel

---

[5] Foley, Frederick W., Ph.D., "Intimacy and Sexuality with Multiple Sclerosis," Multiple Sclerosis Foundation, ©Copyright 2000-2013 Multiple Sclerosis Foundation, All Rights Reserved, www.msfocus.org

problems, fatigue, spasticity, muscle weakness, body or hand tremors and non-genital sensory changes.[6]

"Tertiary sexual dysfunction results from disability-related psychosocial and cultural issues that can interfere with one's sexual feelings and experience."[7]

For sexual problems with men with MS the most frequent treatment is for erectile dysfunction. Oral medications include Viagra®, (sildenafil citrate), Levitra® (vardenafil), and Cialis TM (tadalafil). There are other medications as well. Other more invasive forms of treatment include the surgical implantation of a penile prosthesis but used only as a last resort.[8]

---

[6] *Ibid*
[7] *Ibid*
[8] *Ibid*

For women, "Loss of libido, or sex drive, is the most frequently reported sexual symptom among women with MS. Currently, there are no medicines that are effective for this symptom. There have been case reports that have addressed this topic in MS. In one, sex therapy in combination with MS symptom management and communication skills training, reported anecdotal success in women with MS. Behavioral re-training that targets redevelopment of sexual pleasure in the absence of libido has been reported. The rationale for behavioral re-training is that partially differing neural pathways mediate sexual drive and sexual pleasure or response. In the absence of libido, a different set of behaviors and attitudes are required to stimulate sexual pleasure. In other words, the nervous system is often sufficiently intact to respond to sexual stimulation even when libido is absent. The issue thus becomes one of sexually 'getting started' without libido, which is taught via behavior therapy."[9]

The simplest prescription for vaginal dryness and tightness is the use of water-soluble lubricants. "Similar to the erectile response in men, vaginal lubrication is controlled by multiple pathways in the brain and spinal cord, some of which may be compromised in MS. ... However, most women who use lubricants do not use sufficient amounts. If dryness persists with lubricant use, more generous dosing is needed."[10]

Of possible interest for those who have experienced decrease in libido is "The Multiple Sclerosis Intimacy and Sexuality Questionnaire-19 (MSISQ-19)." It was developed as a "reliable and valid self-report

---

[9] *Ibid*
[10] *Ibid*

questionnaire to assess the perceived influence of Multiple Sclerosis (MS) symptoms on sexual activity and satisfaction and the perceived influence of MS symptoms on the overall quality of intimate relationships."[10]

It is worth noting, "From a research perspective, treatment of orgasmic loss in women with MS has been poorly studied."[11]

At a personal level, Carol's libido had been absent for several years. She was saddened thinking that she would never again experience orgasm.

---

[10] Sanders, Audrey Sorgen, Ph.D., Foley, Frederick W., Ph.D., LaRocca, Nicholas G., Ph.D., and Zemon, Vance, Ph.D. "The Multiple Sclerosis Intimacy and Sexuality Questionnaire-19 (MSISQ-19)," *Sexuality and Disability,* March 2000, Vol. 18, pp. 326
[11] Foley *op cit*

The Sociopathic Unwelcome Guest

Carol was diagnosed with MS in 1978 at age 30. As of this writing she is 68. In 1978 there was no treatment for MS and no disease modifying drugs. When informed of her diagnosis by her neurologist she was told there was nothing that could be done for it. She has relapsing MS. With that kind of MS there may be long periods where the MS is in remission and then flare-ups occur.

When we met December 1987, Carol told me that she had MS but was in good remission with no outward or noticeable symptoms. When people marry, they marry each other with all the baggage each brings to the union. Traditional marriage vows use the exchange of words, containing the promise to love honor and keep her "for better or worse, for richer or poorer, in sickness and in health, and forsaking all others, be faithful only to her, for as long as you both shall live?" Those are wonderful words. "In sickness and in health" and "as long as you both shall live" covers a lot of territory. We cannot predict the future. For us, it has been an amazing pilgrimage.

Nonetheless, MS runs silent and runs deep even in the absence of relapses. It still may be causing damage to the central nervous system, (CNS), causing lesions on the brain and spinal column although there may not be noticeable symptoms for a while.

The first disease modifying drug to come on the market for the treatment of relapsing-remitting MS was Betaseron, in the interferon class of drugs. It was approved for use around 2000. Carol could have been put on the drug at that time but her neurologist never offered it to her. Further, he told her specifically, "Your MS has burned itself out."

As it turns out, MS does not burn itself out as her neurologist had said. In May 2003, as we were preparing for a trip to the Florida Gulf Coast, Carol began experiencing a major MS attack. The sociopath attacked with fury. Before leaving home, Carol called her neurologist's office to set an emergency appointment. She was told that the office no longer had her medical records and she would have to fill out all new paperwork and could not get an appointment until the paperwork was completed. We were told later by a nurse who had worked for that neurologist that he had quit working with MS patients.

We went to San Destin, Florida to a business meeting with Carol in a wheel chair which her primary care doctor helped to obtain. By Memorial Day, the relapse was so severe that we went to the emergency room at the hospital at Fort Walton Beach. We were fortunate in that the attending neurologist's wife had MS, so he was very familiar with the disease. He had been at a barbecue party and came to the bedside in Bermuda shorts. He said at that time that MS never burns itself out.

That MS relapse was particularly debilitating. Carol spent an extended period of time in a wheelchair. She started physical therapy upon our return home to Nashville, Tennessee. She found a new neurologist who gave her information about disease modifying drugs. Carol chose to go on Betaseron and has been on it ever since. As a result of that relapse, the disability became severe on multiple matrices. After getting out of the wheelchair, Carol walked with a cane for a period of time but that was not adequate. She suffered frequent falls. When we knew that the cane was not adequate, she began using a walker and we fitted the house with hand-rails to provide greater safety in the home.

The law of large numbers dictates that the more frequent the falls, the more likely there will be serious injuries. She has hit her head hard at least three times. On two of those occasions she was knocked unconscious. On one occasion she fell face forward at the Frist Center for the Visual Arts and hit her forehead on the marble floor and was knocked unconscious. She was taken to Vanderbilt Medical Center for emergency care. On another occasion she fell backward and struck the back of her head on our hardwood floor so hard that she was knocked unconscious. The blow was so hard her earrings flew off. Again, she was taken to the ER.

On another occasion, Carol fell in the house hitting her shoulder against the wall and suffered a dislocated right shoulder as a result. She was taken to Baptist Hospital where the shoulder was put back in its socket. With arthroscopic surgery three tendons were reattached but one of the tendons failed to remain attached. She went through a long period of having her arm in a sling followed by physical therapy, (PT). The PT restored some of the function of her shoulder but she was left with limited range of motion on her right arm.

As a result of the shoulder injury, Carol was unable to perform the duties of a financial advisor as she was unable to write or drive and could not use the computer. Phone calls were more difficult with just her left arm. That injury effectively ended her career as a financial advisor. We incurred heavy debt for a period of time.

Responding to the oppressive debt, we sharply reduced our spending. In addition, at age 62, I qualified for and we obtained a reverse mortgage which eliminated our mortgage payment. Our finances are now stable. We make ends meet and save money on both our Social Security incomes, my Tennessee State retirement, a church pension and some investment income.

Carol's other falls resulted in two broken wrists, and a fractured shoulder, all of which required ER visits. In addition, there have been other injuries due to lack of dexterity in her hands and fingers. She severely cut her finger with a knife while preparing food in the kitchen. This resulted in another visit to the ER. Beyond that, she fell and hit her eyebrow against the tray holding her computer keyboard causing a gash on her right eye. This required stitches in the ER. On still another occasion, she fell hitting her head against the cabinet under the kitchen sink and totaled the cabinet door, but with no apparent injury to her head.

There have been numerous emergency visits to our home by the Metro-Nashville Fire Department rescue squad. On three occasions during the night, Carol fell to the floor in our bedroom attempting to go from the bed to the bathroom. She was so weak she could not get herself to her feet and I was virtually helpless in assisting her. Getting to her feet was made more difficult due to her right arm being in a sling because of the right shoulder dislocation as noted above. It took three firemen to get her to her feet, safely to the bathroom, and back into bed. On other occasions, when she fell during the transition to the toilet at night, and could not get up, we used a urinal on the floor in order for her to void. On those occasions, she remained on the floor for the night with a pillow from the bed and a blanket to cover her. When she had regained her strength by the morning she could get to her feet with some assistance from me.

On one occasion, Carol fell in the parking lot on her way into a restaurant. It was a particularly hot day and the pavement was scalding. She could not get up. In spite of her cries for help no one heard her or came to her assistance for some time. Eventually a person driving by got help from the restaurant employees who helped her to her feet. We know of one woman with MS who fell in her back yard on a very hot day and could not get to her feet or get help. She died of heat exhaustion.

In all the above situations I felt utterly helpless in getting Carol to her feet and could not simply lift her up as I was not that strong, even though I work out regularly. When I would hear her fall, I always feared the worst. The stress I experienced during those situations was enormous. "Things that go bump in the night" or day programmed me to respond with alarm. I felt helpless.

The difficulty getting Carol to her feet when she fell was worsened due to obesity. She had put on weight over the years. When we met December 1987 she weighed 160 pounds and when we married December 1989 she weighed 145 pounds. Over the years she gained and lost weight but steadily gained weight over time. At one point she weighed 200 pounds. So when she fell, I simply could not get her to her feet.

I tried not to nag Carol on the issue of her excessive weight. My approach from time to time was to ask her to lose the weight for me due to the difficulty getting her to her feet. Health benefits were mentioned as well when we talked about it. However, motivation comes from within. The motivation to lose weight had to be on her terms, not mine. Her motivation to lose weight came on her terms and will be described later.

Of course, excessive weight compounds the disability due to MS and exacerbates fatigue, walking ability and walking distance. Excessive weight places an extra burden on the legs already weakened by MS.

Imagine putting fifty pounds on your back all at once. Anyone, and especially someone with MS would immediately notice difficulty in walking and balance. When we gain weight, the effects are so gradual as to not be noticed but this has the same effect.

Prior to embarking on ST, the range of functions the sociopath stole from Carol included leg strength and the ability to walk any significant distance before the risk of falling. Energy levels have varied. Some of the side effects from the Betaseron injections which she gives herself include flu-like symptoms, muscle weakness and fatigue the following day. Poor balance and coordination were common with her frequently stumbling without falling. Dexterity in her fingers was compromised. Muscle stiffness/spasticity and leg cramps have been common.

She also experienced foot drop, sometimes called

"drop foot." Foot drop is the inability to lift the front part of the foot. "This causes the toes to drag along the ground while walking. To avoid dragging the toes, people with foot drop may also lift their knees higher than normal. Or they may swing the leg in a wide arc. ... In general, foot drop stems from weakness or paralysis of the muscles that lift the foot."[11]

Spasticity and leg cramps were also a problem for Carol. Spasticity has been likened by some as trying to walk in mud. She has also likened it to her legs being stiff as a board. "There are two types of severe MS-related spasticity: In *flexor spasticity,* mostly involving the hamstrings (muscles on the back of the upper leg, and hip flexors (muscles at the top of the upper thigh), the hips and

---

[11] WebMD, Reviewed by Rinku Chatterjee, MD on February 20, 2012, ©2012, WebMd, LLC. All rights reserved.

knees are bent and difficult to straighten. In *extensor spasticity,* involving the quadriceps and adductors (muscles on the front and inside of the upper leg), the hips and knees remain straight with the legs very close together or crossed over at the ankles."[12]

Carol's spasticity was from her thighs to her feet. Cramping occurred primarily in her feet. In addition to medication, treatment for spasticity includes physical and occupational therapy and surgical measures for those rare cases of spasticity that defy all other treatment. In addition, non-pharmacologic interventions include stretching, leg braces, and range of motion exercises. "General conditioning can also help to strengthen weak and deconditioned muscle groups and increase endurance and cardiovascular conditioning. Strengthening can be

---

[12] National Multiple Sclerosis Society

achieved in a variety of ways, using free weights, machines, therabands, Swiss Balls, or aquatic exercises. Strength training can also assist the timing of movements, depending on the strength or weakness of the agonist/antagonist muscles."[14]

"Shit happens."*

Loss of bladder and bowel control was very problematic. Carol frequently peed on herself, sometimes in public situations. She experienced bowel problems with constipation on the one hand and loose bowls on the other hand. She had frequent episodes of fecal incontinence which I call, "projectile pooping."

*Seen on car bumper stickers

[14] Emrich, Lisa, Health Guide Tuesday, March 24, 2009, www.HealthCentral.com, *How to manage MS-Related Spasticity*, Source: *Spasticity* by Sue Kushner, MS, PT and Kathi Brandfass, MS, PT, Clinical Bulletin/Information for Health Professionals. © 2004 National Multiple Sclerosis Society

Of course, I had to clean up the mess. All these episodes caused me considerable stress. One of the neurologists who speaks regularly to the MS support groups which we attend said that many people who experience loss of bladder and bowel control become virtually homebound because of the fear of losing control of elimination in public. Carol and I had that justifiable fear. Beyond that her disability was increasing on multiple scales.

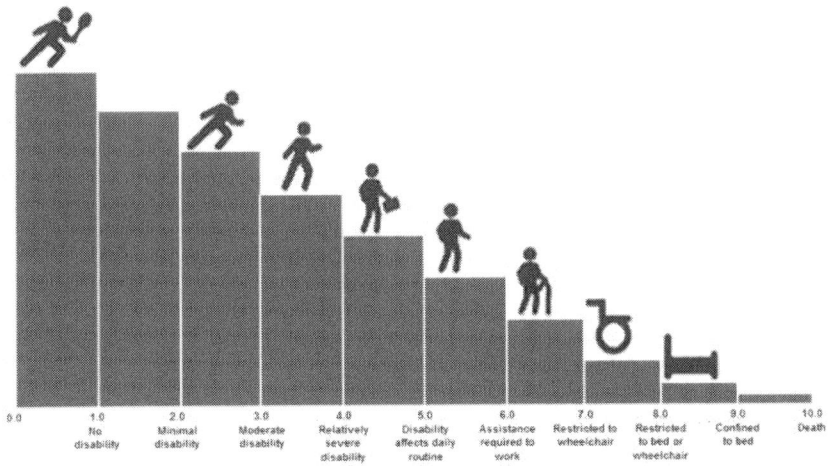

Expanded Disability Status Scale (EDSS)[13]

On the Expanded Disability Status Scale (EDSS), the following systems are compromised: Pyramidal (ability to walk), Cerebellar (coordination), brainstem, sensory (touch), bowel and bladder, visual, and cerebral. The pyramidal scale rates the ability to walk on a 10 point scale.

---

[13] Kurtzke, John F., "Rating neurologic impairment in multiple sclerosis: an expanded disability status scale, (EDSS)," *Neurology* 33 (11): 1444-52

Normal begins at 0.0. Being helpless in bed but able to communicate and eat is 9.0. Death due to MS is 10.0. The limitation of the chart is that it does not measure coordination, touch, bowel and bladder, visual, cerebral/cognition, fatigue, sexuality and other forms of MS disability. Those need to be measured clinically and by self-monitoring.

Before we began Carol's ST regimen, she would have rated 6.5, constant bilateral support, (cane, crutch, walker or braces) required to walk 20 meters without resting. Since starting ST 1/1/12, by our estimates, as of 12/19/14, the date of this writing, she would be rated 6.0, Intermittent or unilateral constant assistance (cane, crutch, walker or braces) required to walk 100 meters with or without resting. She can walk that distance, and more, without resting. Since beginning ST, she has also improved on cerebellar, sensory, bowel and bladder functions, and in other multiple kinds of ways.

## Issues of Aging

Loss of muscle mass is a major contributor to disability in both the Pyramidal and Cerebellar systems. One way this occurs is through normal aging in the absence of weight bearing exercises. This is known as sarcopenia.[14] It is further noted that, "Inactive aging is associated with significant amounts of muscle loss on a year-by-year basis. Adults who do not perform some type of strength training sacrifice more than 5 pounds of muscle tissue every

---

[14]Bemben, Michael G., Ph.D., FACSM, "The physiology of aging: what you can do to slow or stop the loss of muscle mass – Research," for the American College of Sports Medicine's (ACSM) February 2001, Current Comment, Copyright 2002 Aerobics and Fitness Association of America, Copyright 2002 Gale Group, American Fitness, May-June 2002

decade, and older adults lose even more than that."[15] It is further noted, that on average, a "woman over 25 years old who *doesn't* do strength-training exercises loses about one-half pound of muscle each year, or roughly 5 pounds in a decade, research has found. That makes you feel weaker and look flabbier, and results in about a 3% decrease in resting metabolic rate (RMR). Over time, this slowing metabolism can lead to an increase in body fat."[16] What this means over the long term is that from age 25 to 65 people who do not do strength training will lose 20 pounds of muscle mass. While losing muscle mass, most

---

[15] Westcott, Wayne, PhD., Training consultant for the US Navy, ACE, the YMCA of the USA, and Nautilus, ZENFIT, posted August 21, 2011 by Bar Wagar.
[16] Matthews, Jessica, MS, E-RYT, Exercise Physiologist, American Council of Exercise, "Best Strength-Training Exercises for Women," *Lifescript Healthy Living for Women,* 3/21/2012

Americans gain fat. These factors, coupled with MS, make walking disability more likely.

Another factor contributing to MS disease progression and disability in women is menopause. Research has demonstrated that link. "Dr. Riley Bove, recipient of a Clinician Scientist Development Award, co-sponsored by the (MS) Society and/the American Brain Foundation, gathered information on MS during menopause from 391 women enrolled in a large-scale, long term study at Brigham and Women's Hospital in Boston. The results show that disease progression changed at or around menopause toward a more rapid accumulation of disability. Further research will determine whether hormonal shifts are responsible, which may lead to a solution for women with MS going through menopause."[17]

The benefits of exercise in the form of walking and moderate weight training have been demonstrated to significantly reduce "the chance that a frail older person will become physically disabled, according to one of the largest and longest-running studies of its kind to date. ...

'For the first time, we have directly shown that exercise can effectively lesson or prevent the development of physical disability in a population of extremely vulnerable elderly people,' said Dr. Marco Pahor, the

---

[17] "Hormones and gender under the microscope" *Momentum*, Fall 2014

director of the Institute on Ageing at the University of Florida in Gainesville and the lead author of the study. ...

The exercise group received information about aging but also started a program of walking and light, lower-body weight training with ankle weights, going to the research center twice a week for supervised group walks on a track, with the walks growing progressively longer. They were also asked to complete three or four more exercise sessions at home, aiming for a total of 150 minutes of walking and about three 10-minute sessions of weight-training exercises each week."[18]

---

[18] Reynolds, Gretchen, "To Age Well, Walk, *The New York Times*, May 27, 2014

Brain shrinkage is associated with aging, particularly in the hippocampus, the memory center of the brain. One study in the *Los Angeles Times* reported, "To complete the study, the team recruited 120 older people who didn't exercise regularly. Half were randomly assigned to an aerobic exercise program … The group doing aerobic exercise had increases in hippocampus volume: up 2.12 percent in the left hippocampus, and 1.97 percent in the right hippocampus."[19] Compare this with the group that didn't exercise. "Also according to the study, the people in the control group who didn't exercise saw an average of 1.4 percent *decrease* in hippocampus size."[20]

---

[19] "Exercise: A Simple Way to Radically Increase Your Brain Power," Fitness Peak, Mercola.com, March 7, 2011
[20] *Ibid*

Another risk facing those with MS is osteoporosis, which is the loss of bone mass. The risk of breaking bones when falling is greater in the presence of osteoporosis. While also affecting males, "The disease is a major health threat for aging females, affecting about 8 million of the 10 million osteoporosis sufferers in the U.S. One in three women over 50 get fractures resulting from osteoporosis. Another 34 million have osteopenia, a precursor of the disease." [21] It is further noted, there are 300,000 hip fractures per year. "About 24% of hip-fracture patients and a third of elderly men with hip fractures die within a year, often because they can't regain mobility."[22] One of the ways to ensure healthy bones is ST. Dr. Edward C. Geehr recommends several ways to ensure healthy bones, one of

---

[21] Geehr, Edward C., M.D., Lifescript Chief Medical Officer, '7 Tips For Healthy Bones if You're Over 30," *Lifescript Healthy Living for Women,* 12/20/2013
[22] *Ibid*

which is ST. "Strength training with weight-bearing exercises (such as walking, jogging and dancing) helps prevent or slow progression of osteoporosis. Strength training increases the tug of muscles on the bones and weight-bearing exercise also stresses bones, which keep them strong."[23] Resistance training exercises may be done at home. "Lisa Reale Munn, a certified personal trainer, said, 'It's super important for women to incorporate resistance training into their weekly regimen to protect and strengthen their bones as well as maintain and protect their bodies, organs and overall health.'"[24] The risk of disability increases with normal aging due to loss of muscle and bone mass. Coupled with MS in the absence of ST, the

---

[23] *Ibid*

[24] Munn, Lisa Reale, "Resistance Training at Home," *The Tennessean,* January 9, 2014

risk of disability increases. Since this is the case, ST is essential for bone health.

Excess body fat acerbates disability in walking. Couple excess body weight with MS and disability will be more severe. It should be noted that increase in muscle mass increases the body's ability to burn calories and fat.

ST is the way to increase muscle mass.

In Carol's experience we had become desperate. So, what did we do and what can be done about it?

Chapter 2: What We Did

"What does not kill me, makes me stronger."[25]

---

[25]Nietzsche, Friedrich, *Twilight of the Idols,* 1888

When I worked as a chaplain at Middle Tennessee Mental Health Institute in Nashville, the Clinical Director said, "Patients are responsible for their illness." This does not mean the patient caused the illness. Rather, it means the person with an illness is responsible for it. In healthy relationships with doctors, the patient and doctor work as a team but the patient is responsible for the illness. I believe that is true for Carol and anyone with MS, or anyone else with any disease.

In my years of playing college football, in the early sixties, I learned a great deal about ST. A basic assumption is that, high weights and low repetitions create the most muscle mass.

When we began, we started our workout regimen at home. With Carol holding on to a hand rail for balance, she did simple squats, strengthening the quadriceps.

Standing with the balls of her feet on a 2 X 4 board, she did calf raises, strengthening the calf muscles.

After we had been doing those simple set of exercises, Carol had a follow-up exam with Dr. Shan-Ren Zhou, her neurologist. On exam, Dr. Zhou pressed his hand against her thigh while she lifted her thigh against the pressure of his hand. This tests the strength of the *Ileus Soleus*. When Dr. Zhou conducted the test, he jerked his head back in surprise. He wanted to know what she had been doing. We told him she was doing ST.

We proceeded forward with some basic assumptions. I assume the patient is responsible for his or her illness. I assume that an increase in muscle mass will make up for some of the deficits in neurology. I assumed that we would increase muscle mass with *aggressive* ST from neck to feet coupled with flexibility exercises from neck to feet. I assume that we must listen to the body and the body does not lie. I assume we must "do no harm," an essential tenet of medicine.

I further assume all exercises are not alike or created equal and that ST is the preferred exercise over aerobic and other exercises for those with MS. This is not to denigrate aerobic exercise or water aerobics for those with MS but they do not do as much to increase muscle mass as does ST. Aerobic exercises also raise body heat which may induce fatigue faster than ST and flexibility training alone. Bike riding may increase muscle mass in the quadriceps and calves and improve cardiovascular health but does not strengthen other major muscle groups from neck to feet to the same degree as ST and flexibility training. Further, if bike riding, walking or running are done outside, particularly in warm weather, then that will have a debilitating effect due to heat. Even if these are done in an air-conditioned environment then body temperature will rise. The downside to aerobic training is that for someone with MS, their legs will become like wet noodles.

## Cognition, Memory and Exercise

Multiple studies support exercise and in particular ST to help cognitive functions and memory in aging adults. Walking appears to help memory in older adults. Also, researchers studied women ages 70 to 80 with mild cognitive impairment, (MCI), who were divided into one of three groups, ST, aerobic training or balance-and-tone training. At the end of the study period they found that those who participated in ST fared best. They outperformed the other groups on measuring attention, memory and higher-order brain functions like conflict resolution. They also showed increased function in three brain regions involved in memory.[23] Other studies found similar results. "In conclusion, our study suggests that twice-weekly RT is a promising strategy to alter the trajectory of cognitive decline in seniors with mild cognitive impairment."[24] Another study found ST giving a boost to seniors' brains. As both aging and MS progress, the risk to cognitive functions grows over time. One study focused on women between 70 and 80 years old who had

---

[23] Sifferlin, Alexandra, "Mind Your Reps: Exercise, Especially Weight Lifting, Helps Keep the Brain Sharp," Healthland.Time.com

[24] Nagamatsu, Lindsay S, MA; Handy, Todd C., PhD; Hsu, C. Liang, BSc; Voss, Michelle, PhD; Liu-Ambrose, Teresa, PT, PhD; "Resistance Training Promotes Cognitive and Functional Brain Plasticity in Seniors With Probable Mild Cognitive Impairment," JAMA Network/JAMA Internal Medicine, April 23, 2012, Vol. 172. No. 8

complained of memory difficulties and were deemed to have "probable" MCI. The women were randomly assigned to a ST program that included lifting weights, one-third walked outdoors in an aerobics program, and one-third took basic balance and toning classes. "After 6 months, compared to those in the balance/tone classes, the strength-training group was found to have experienced 'significant' cognitive improvement. The Strength-training group also experienced activity changes in three specific parts of the brain's cortex associated with cognitive behavior, the researchers found. These changes were not seen among the balance/tone group."[26]

One of the important cognitive functions affected by MS is memory. "Almost 60 percent of people with

---

[26] Mozes, Alan, Health Day Reporter, "Strength Training May Give Boost to Seniors' Brains." Health Day, *U.S. News,* 4/23/2012

multiple sclerosis experience some sort of memory problems, according to the National Multiple Sclerosis Society. More rarely, in about 5 to 10 percent of people with MS, memory becomes limited to the point that it significantly interferes with daily function."[27]

All of this is even more crucial as the risk of developing secondary progressive MS increases with age even in the absence of new brain or spinal lesions seen on MRI exam. Dr. Harold Moses, M.D., a well-known neurologist and MS researcher at Vanderbilt University, indicates there is a fifty-fifty chance that there will be secondary progression of the disease after age sixty-five even with disease modifying drugs. ST holds promise to delay or even reverse disability due to secondary progressive MS.

---

[27] "12 Ways to Improve Memory with MS," Everydayhealth.com © 2014, Last Updated 01/08/2014

The memory center of the brain is the hippocampus. It is noted that "Hippocampal volume shrinks 1-2% annually in older adults without dementia, and this loss of volume increases the risk for developing cognitive impairment."[28] This study by Erickson, *et al*, found that aerobic exercise training increases hippocampal volume; hippocampal volume is related to improvements in spatial memory; and BDNF, a mediator of neurogenesis in the dentate gyrus.[29]

Another study showed that exercise appears to reduce the risk for common age-associated disorders including Alzheimer's disease (AD). "ABSTRACT Lifestyle

---

[28]Erickson, Kirk I.; Voss, Michelle W.; Prakash, Ruchika Shaurya; Szabo, Amanda; Chaddock, Laura; Kim, Jannifer S.; Heo, Susie; Alves, Heloisa; White, Siobhan M.; Wojcicki, Thomas R.; Mailey, Emily; Vieira, Victoria J.; Martin, Stephen A.; Pence, Brandt D.; Woods, Jeffrey A.; McAuley, Edward; and Kramer, Arthur F., "Exercise training increases size of hippocampus and improves memory," PNAS, February 15, 2011, Vol. 108, No. 7, pp. 3017-3022

[29] *Ibid*

factors such as intellectual stimulation, cognitive and social engagement, nutrition, and various types of exercise appear to reduce the risk for common age-associated disorders such as Alzheimer's disease (AD) and vascular dementia. In fact, many studies have suggested that promoting physical activity can have a protective effect against cognitive deterioration later in life. Slowing or a deterioration of walking speed is associated with poor performance in tests assessing psychomotor speed and verbal fluency in elderly individuals. Fitness training influences a wide range of cognitive processes, and the largest positive impact observed is for executive (a.k.a. frontal lobe) functions such as tasks mediated by the hippocampus and result in major changes in plasticity in the hippocampus."[30]

In addition, the hippocampus is linked to the limbic system including the hypothalamus. With many important connections, "The hypothalamus has centers involved in sexual function, endocrine function, behavioral function and autonomic control."[31] The hypothalamus requires several types of inputs including olfaction, the viscera and the retina. It influences many functions including autonomics, and endocrine functions and behaviors. The endocrine functions have direct axonal connections to the posterior pituitary gland (vasopressin and oxytocin control) or via release of releasing factors

---

[30] Foster, FP, Rosenblatt, KP, et al, "Exercise-Induced Cognitive Plasticity, Implications for Mild Cognitive Impairment and Alzheimer's Disease," PubMed

[31] Swenson, Rand, DC, MD, PhD, Dartmouth Medical School, Editor, Chapter 9- Limbic System, *Review of Clinical and Functional Neuroscience, Copyright* © Swenson 2006

into the hypothalamic-hypophyseal portal system (to influence anterior pituitary function.)[32]

The pituitary, known as the "master glad," regulates the other glands of the body. Among other things, the pituitary gland regulates hair growth with the follicle-stimulating hormone (FSH), the testes and ovaries, and oxytocin.[33]

One of the hormones that neurotransmitters send from the Deep Limbic System is oxytocin. "Oxytocin promotes bonding and attachment and if all the hormones had an opportunity to vote for the 'most popular' award in the hormone yearbook, its peers would vote for it every

---

[32] *Ibid*

[33] Shirley, Wayne, "What Are the Functions of the Pituitary and Thyroid Glands?" ehow contributor, References – University of Maryland Medical Center: Endocrinology Health Guide; Resources – "How the Endocrine System Works," J. Matthew Neal, 2001

time because it makes others feel good and close when it is active.

For the Psychology student, here is the scientific description: 'Oxytocin is produced mainly in the hypothalamus (which is in the Deep Limbic System part of the brain), where it is either released into blood via the pituitary gland, or to other parts of the brain and spinal cord, where it binds to oxytocin receptors to influence behavior and physiology.' (DAngelis (http://.apa.org/monitor/feb08/oxytocin.aspx))."[34]

Exercise, and we maintain, ST in particular, creates positive changes in the brain as noted above. How this worked with Carol will be described later.

---

[34] Sands, Bryan A., "Sex and Glue: The Emotional Bond of a Physical Act," from radio interview and blog, June 23, 2013

## The Road to Reversal of MS Disability

Carol started the aggressive ST at the Maryland Farms YMCA in Brentwood, with me as her strength trainer, on January 2, 2012. After the first exercise session, she was so fatigued that she laid her head down on the table in the Subway restaurant in the Y and fell asleep. One of the Y staff was so concerned that they asked her if anything was wrong. Walking back to the car she had to stop and sit on a chair outside the Y lobby before continuing her trek to the car.

In spite of the initial fatigue as just described, Carol began to notice positive results in just a few days. We continued on by increasing weights on the combination of resistance machines and free weights.

## Workout Rationale

Our workout rationale is based on four assumptions. First, the brain and the body, including the muscular-skeletal system, are an integrated system. Everything works together. Therefore, arms, core and legs, including the ankles, must all be strengthened.

Arms and core are important for balance and, in the event of a fall, are important on getting to one's feet. Leg strength is important to increase walking distance, improve balance and get to one's feet in the event of a fall.

Second, when a particular sub/system is worked it must include all the muscle groups. For instance, in working the legs, it is not good enough to work just the quads and calf muscles. You must also strengthen the adductors and abductors and the muscles which control the ankles/feet.

Third, balance and coordination are a combination of many factors. Muscle mass and muscle strength is one of those important factors. Evidence already cited indicates that people who did ST fared better than those who did aerobics, conditioning, balance and toning exercises only.

Fourth, the smooth muscles controlling bowel and bladder functions must be strengthened as well. This requires a consistent, and regular incorporation of Kegel exercises into the workout routine.

## Strength Gains

The gains in strength as measured by the amount of weight pushed have been enormous for Carol. Those gains in strength translate to positive gains as measured by multiple matrices which will be described in the next section.

On all workouts we drink ice water. Water is needed for hydration but ice water is needed to cool the body through the core. A set of ST exercises does increase body temperature but ice water helps cool the core. Also, the rest between sets allows the body to cool on its own.

On Sundays and Tuesdays we work arms and core with back extensions, dead lifts and abdominal crunches. On Monday and Wednesday we do legs and core. On Tuesday and Thursday mornings Carol works out with a personal trainer for a half hour. That exercise group is composed mostly of people with MS plus one with Cerebral Palsy. We do flexibility/stretching exercises every day neck to feet. We do core and flexibility/stretching only on Fridays. If we miss a Sunday through Wednesday workout then we make up what we missed on Friday. We keep a Strength Workout Record for each workout.

To begin with the exercises were a combination of free weights with dumbbells and barbells with me spotting her and some exercise machines. We have since changed to almost all exercise machines since they are easier to use. The one dumbbell exception is concentration curls for the biceps. We do three sets unless she experiences excessive fatigue and then move it down to one or two sets.

We listen to Carol's body. If she experiences sharp pain in an exercise then we stop. Sharp pain is different from the "burn" of muscle fatigue after a number of repetitions. If she is particularly fatigued or weak, which is rare, then we may reduce the number of sets to one or two. We always finish with floor and standing stretching exercises from neck to feet. Beginning December 2014 we added

Pilates to our regimen. We total 8 hours of exercise a week on average unless our schedule is interrupted.

Our first existing record is April 5, 2012 which reflects gains from January 2nd but that record can't be located. The gains on muscle strength as measured by weight pushed are noteworthy. Lateral Pull Down on 4/5/12 was 45 pounds and 17 repetitions, (reps). On 11/30/14 it was 85 pounds and 9 reps. Seated Press on 4/5/12 was 15 pounds and 7 reps. On 11/30/14 it was 40 pounds and 13 reps. On 4/10/12 on Bench Press with barbell and me spotting it was 20 pounds and 22 reps. On 3/4/14 it was 50 pounds and 9 reps. Seated dumbbell lateral raises on 4/5/12 went from 3 pounds 14 reps to 10 pounds 10 reps on 11/30/14 on a machine. Seated dumbbell bicep curls on 4/5/12 went from 5 pounds 14 reps to 10 pounds and 8 reps as a concentration curl on 12/02/14. Abdominal Crunches went from 30 pounds and 13 reps on 4/5/12 to 45 pounds and 8 reps on 3/14/14. Lower Back Extensions went from 75 pounds and 30 reps with one set on 4/5/12 to 145 pounds and 11 reps with full extension and 3 sets on 11/30/14.

Similar results are noted on the leg exercises. The Seated Leg Press went from 245 pounds and 23 reps on 4/9/12 to 400 pounds and 11 reps on 12/03/14. Seated Leg Curls went from 45 pounds and 30 reps on 4/9/2012 to 105 pounds and 7 reps on 12/03/14. Calf raises went from 10 pounds and 10 reps on 4/9/12 to 110 pounds and 7 reps on 12/03/14. Seated Hip Adduction, which works the inner hips and thighs, went from 60 pounds and 20 reps on 4/9/12 to 90 pounds and 11 reps on 12/03/14. Seated Hip Abduction, which works the outer thighs, went from 35 pounds and 10 reps on 4/9/12 to 60 pounds and 13 reps on

3/5/14. It is noteworthy that on the adduction/adduction machine, Carol could not get her legs over the leg pads without my assistance on 4/9/12. She simply did not have enough strength in her *Ileus Soleus* muscle. The *Ileus Soleus* lifts the leg either in a standing or sitting position. All of the time she can now lift her legs over the leg pads without my assistance.

On March 3, 2014 we added the Leg Lift machine to work the *Ileus Soleus,* Carol does leg lifts in which she lifts her legs bent at the knees with her elbows on an elbow rest. As of 12/01/14 she did 13 lifts with both legs and three sets. Prior to this Carol could not lift herself into a position to do leg lifts and did not have the strength to lift her legs. She now has the ability to get into position and lifts both legs at the same time for three sets. The results were seen that day as she was able to get her legs into her pants with greater ease. She also can lift her legs with greater ease into the car, and her walking ease has improved. This progress continues.

## Flexibility Gains

We do two levels of flexibility and stretching exercises from neck to feet following the ST. We hold each stretch for thirty seconds. We do a full set of floor exercises followed by standing exercises.

When we began floor exercises it was often a struggle even using the hand rail of the staircase to come to a standing position. The floor exercises include stretching of the buttocks by pulling the knees to chest. We stretch the hamstring seated with legs on the floor reaching toward the feet. Early on, I noticed she could not point her feet upward while lying down. Rather, her feet flopped outward indicating foot drop.

Following stretching on the floor, Carol does thirty reps of Kegel exercises of bladder and anal sphincters alternately contracting and relaxing those muscles for 30 contractions. We finish the floor routine with isometric exercises in which I hold her feet down while she pushes against my pressure in both directions laterally and upward. We do three sets for a forty second count. This part of the floor exercise is designed for and has proven effective in reversing foot drop. She now can point her feet upward toward the ceiling when we do floor exercises.

## Multiple Clinical Gains Reversing Disability

There have been multiple gains, all reversing different areas of disability. All have improved her and my quality of life. The ability to walk longer distances before fatigue and risk of failure has increased dramatically. The Thigh Lift has improved getting her leg into her pants and into our car from both sides without struggle. All the time

Carol can lift her legs on her own over the pads on the Abduction/Adduction machine without my assistance. In addition, she can lift her leg to a two foot rail for stretching in the gym where she works out with the group of MS people led by Carter Hayes who provides the class *pro bono.* This is something she could not do previously.

It is noted that regarding foot drop, according to WebMd, previously cited, treatments include light-weight braces, shoe inserts (orthotics), physical therapy and surgery.[35] ST was not listed as a treatment. Also, long-term use of braces, while helping with foot drop, will lead to loss of muscle mass in the long run. Also, PT is time-limited and surgery is very invasive and expensive. On the other hand, our use of isometric exercises has totally eliminated foot drop with Carol.

---

[35] WebMD, *op cit*

Significantly, Carol has gained control over bladder and bowels. There have not been any more episodes of "projectile pooping" and only rare and minor episodes of peeing on herself. The only time she has peed on herself is when she has had a urinary tract infection. The full regimen for bladder and bowel control includes a prescription for Detrol, an over-the-counter stool softener, psyllium fiber capsules, either store brand or Metamucil, and two fingers high of prune juice at breakfast. The key for control came with the addition of thirty contractions daily of Kegel exercises. She does Kegel contractions every time we do flexibility/stretching exercises.

While Carol still falls from time to time, she falls less frequently. She did have one hard fall in which she was knocked unconscious on October 29, 2014. She was taken to ER at Williamson County Medical Center. The CT scan was negative and she was not admitted to the hospital.

Carol also fell on December 22, 2014 and was knocked unconscious when her head struck the floor. After regaining consciousness, she was able to get to her feet and sit in a chair. When the ambulance personal arrived she was conscious but her short-term memory was impaired. One the medics did a simple mental status exam and she could not name the president of the United States, could not name the date and could not remember how she fell.

When Carol does fall she is able to get up on her own almost all the time without assistance from others. When she falls, the ST exercises in her arms and core have resulted in her ability to rise unassisted to her feet.

An additional gain has been in the range of motion of Carol's right arm which was limited due to her shoulder dislocation which was mentioned earlier. Since one tendon remained unattached following orthoscopic surgery her range of motion remained limited. With full range of motion a person can reach over the top of the head to the opposite side of the head reaching the ear on the opposite side. During the PT, I was concerned that the therapist was not doing enough ST. PT ended when there was no further improvement. She could only reach her right ear with right hand. With our ST and flexibility exercises she can now reach the top of her head with her right hand. This helps in activities of daily living including being able to reach over to pull the door handle on the passenger side of the car. From the driver's side of her car she can reach over to the glove compartment which she could not do previously.

Also, as she is seated next to the bathroom counter near the sink, she can reach the shelf where her pills are kept in order to dose her weekly pill regimen. The seated vertical press has contributed to that improvement. She can do full extensions with her right arm on that machine for about five reps before failure reduces her range of motion on that side. In addition, the lateral dumbbell raise has helped by strengthening deltoids and trapezium.

Carol never has cramping in her feet. Spasticity only occurs on rare occasions after her Betaseron shot. Her walking is not stiff-legged and is more normal. Her legs are no longer stiff as a board. In addition to Baclefen, but most importantly, we attribute these improvements to ST coupled with flexibility exercises.

Carol has also shown improvements in dexterity in her hands and fingers. We attribute that to the ST in that her forearms are stronger and gripping the bars strengthens her hand muscles. One example of that is that she can now push down the button on the mousse dispenser when she does her hair. This is something she could not do earlier in the ST regimen. In addition, she doesn't drop things as often. Plus, she noticed that at dinner she could cut up her meat with greater ease.

Another improvement is being able to stand without assistance from a grab-bar when she rises from the toilet seat. Getting out of a chair or sofa can be done without struggling. She is able to get up out of a rocking chair without assistance where she sits as a volunteer working with young children at Martha O'Brien Community Center.

Another important gain has been that Carol can move her right foot from the accelerator to the car brake more easily. We attribute this to the isometric exercises we do on her feet. This makes her automobile driving safer.

Other gains include being able to walk up stairs with greater ease and walking with a more upright posture. The improvement in posture would be attributed to the back extension exercise with full range of motion on each repetition. We also do an elbow plank exercise which strengthens the lower back. We added floor Pilates on December 2, 2014 for further strengthening of the core.

Importantly, Carol can transfer from the bed to the toilet at night without fear of falling. This has never happened since these gains. Also, she can sit through a whole movie without fear of peeing on herself before getting to the ladies room.

It is worth noting that core strengthening has proven efficacious for people with MS. "A recent study has shown that people with MS can have significantly reduced balance even when they have no problems with walking.

One element of balance is the ability to maintain a steady trunk whilst moving a limb. When we reach out an arm or take a step to walk, or nervous system switches on our muscles in a specific order, with trunk muscles contracting before limb muscles. The deepest abdominal muscle, transversus abdominis, switches on first in order to stiffen the trunk, followed milliseconds later by muscles that brace the trunk against the direction of limb movement. This stabilizes the body, ensuring that we are not pulled off balance by the moving arm or leg. This trunk steadiness is commonly known as 'core stability.' ...

People with MS have been found to have reduced trunk stability during arm movements, and individuals with delayed activation of trunk muscles have reduced balance. ...

All therapists involved were specialist neurological physiotherapists developed for the project, and the physiotherapist chose a few of these exercises to address the specific needs of each participant. The aim was to improve postural awareness, balance, confidence and functional mobility. The exercises were progressed as ability improved. Participants also did 15 minutes of these same exercise at home each day. …

There was variability in how the participants responded to the core stability training. Five people clearly benefited, with improvement in seven of the nine measures. These showed improved walking speed, better balance while reaching forward and to the side, improved balance standing on one leg, and less difficulty carrying a drink while walking. One further participant gained some benefit, with improvement in four of the measures, while two people did not appear to gain any benefit."[36]

---

[36] Gear, Margaret, Neurophysiotherapist; Hunter, Helen, Clinical Specialist Neurophysiotherapist; Freeman, Jenny, Dr., Reader in Physiotherapy and Rehabilitation, on behalf of Therapists in MS Research Group, "Core stability training in MS," Open Door – February 2011 , pages 8-9, Multiple Sclerosis Trust, all content © 2004-2013

The ST has also paid off with apparent strengthening of her bone mass. Carol began taking Fosamax for osteopenia upon diagnosis by her endocrinologist. She was on Fosamax for five or six years and went off the medication in 2007. When she quit the medication the osteopenia was under control and her bone mass was within normal limits. Upon her most recent examination July 31, 2014, her bone density was well within normal limits in spite of being off medication for seven years. Upon seeing the bone density screening result, the endocrinologist exclaimed, "Wow! He attributes the continuing normal bone density to her ST for over two years.

In addition, Carol does not need to take a nap after exercise. In the past, she would have to take a nap to recover strength and energy after a workout.

Another interesting change has been an improvement in Carol's vision. For some time, in addition to her contact lenses, she used reading glasses for near vision. Upon her last eye exam by her optometrist on January 23, 2014, he said that near vision had improved and she no longer needed reading glasses. My ophthalmologist indicated that cataracts could improve near vision. However, Carol does not have cataracts.

Coupled with the improvement in near vision, Carol's sense of smell has improved as well. She has increased ability in the olfactory system.

The most surprising change has been the resurrection of Carol's libido. Over more than a decade there had been a decline of sexual interest and the ability to experience sexual pleasure and orgasm. She had come to believe that she would never again be able to experience orgasm and was saddened by that prospective loss.

The week of January 12, 2014 and very rapidly on January 18th she began to notice a return of sexual interest and pleasure in sex to the point of being able to again experience orgasm. Prior to this there were indications changes were occurring in this area in that she began to experience nocturnal erotic dreams to the point or orgasm.

Prior to this change, we would rate Carol's sexual desire and ability to enjoy sex as a 3 on a 10 point scale. On the 18$^{th}$ this moved rapidly to a 10. To use an analogy, she became revived from a "near death" experience of her sexuality. She continues to stay horny as the date of this writing.

Coupled with this change, Carol's mood improved. She has never been depressive. Since this change her mood moved from a 7 to a 10 without evidence of mania.

Also, amazingly, Carol's total testosterone level went to 670.9 ng/dl on lab results of 7/29/14. This is in spite of the fact that at age 68 she is post-menopausal. Her primary care physician responded that her testosterone level was higher than his. Her neurologist, Dr. Zhou responded with surprise when told her total testosterone reading. The average adult female testosterone level is 15-70 ng/dl.[37]

The role of testosterone in females is well-documented. "According to Dr. Susan Rako, testosterone is not the exclusive domain of men and is every bit as much a sex hormone for women as it is for the other gender.

---

[37] Severson, Alexia, "Testosterone Levels by Age," Medically reviewed by George Krucik, MD, MBA, Copyright © 2005-2014 Healthline Networks, Inc.

When testosterone levels dip because of menopause, Dr. Rako maintains that a woman can experience a 'flatness' of mood, brittle hair, dry skin, loss of muscle strength and tone. Her sex drive may fall by the wayside and she may have less sensitivity in her genitals and nipples. Testosterone is needed to help maintain a woman's bone density as well as assist in the health of a woman's vulva and enabling the regrowth of clitoral tissue. Our brains work better when we have sufficient

levels of testosterone."[38]

It should be noted that, "Too much testosterone can also cause problems. One common effect of high testosterone levels for women is hirsutism, the growth of

---

[38] Pearce, eHow Contributor, "the Role of Testosterone in Females," eHow

excessive facial or body hair. Male pattern baldness is also possible."[39]

Changes that have occurred sexually for Carol include increased sexual arousal daily. She stays horny. This is coupled with increased vaginal lubrication upon arousal. She is easily orgasmic as well. Typically we have sex one to three times a day.

One other effect of the return of sexuality is excessive hair growth on her face and body. The hair is not coarse and dark as is typical of hirsutism but dark and soft. It is noted that, "Women normally produce low levels of male hormones (androgens). If your body makes too much of this hormone, you may have unwanted hair growth."[40] This

---

[39]Gaudet, Henry; Edited by A. Joseph; wise GEEK, Last Modified July 16, 2014

[40] Tabif, TP, Hair diseases. In: Habif, TP, ed., *Clinical Dermatology*, 5th ed., St. Louis, MO, Mosby Elsevier, 3009, Chapter 24, Medicine Plus

condition could be "Hyperthecosis (a condition in which the ovaries produce too much male hormones.)"[41]

As previously noted, the pituitary gland regulates hair growth with the follicle stimulating hormone, FSH. As noted on the lab report of 7/29/14, the optimal FSH is 3.5-12.5. Carol's FSH was 41.7 mIU/mL, well over the optimal upper limit. I would appear that her elevated FSH has contributed to her excessive hair growth.

She is having her facial hair removed with laser treatment. This is proving effective.

As described previously in the link of exercise and in particular ST on the limbic system it seems reasonable that the improvement in vision, olfaction, bone mass and libido were the result of the ST work we have been doing.

---

[41] *Ibid*

The link between exercise and libido in women has been supported in other research. "New research confirms that women who hit the gym have a better time in bed. In a study from the University of Texas at Austin, women with low sex drive (caused by prescription drugs) who worked out regularly for 21 days reported higher sexual desire – especially when they had sex after a workout. Their exercise related improvement in genital bloodflow is probably a result women not on meds can also expect, researchers say."[42]

This certainly has been the case with Carol. Her libido is highest upon completing a workout. I suggest that this is in area for future research with a larger number of study participants. As noted earlier, "treatment of orgasmic loss in women with MS has been poorly studied."

---

[42] "Heat Up Her Cooldown" *Men's Health,* April 2014, p. 40

One of the other gains for Carol which appears correlated with the return of libido is that her sleep has improved. She now sleeps soundly through the night, only occasionally needing to get up to go to the bathroom.

## Losing Weight

One of the collateral benefits of the resurrection of Carol's libido is that it has become the motivating force in her losing weight. Motivation for anything hinges on the "why" of wanting to change or do something positive. For her the why was the link between feeling sexual and sexy and having a slender body and looking sexy. The "how" of change follows from the why.

Part of losing weight is creating more muscle mass through ST. More muscle mass is needed to lose weight in that muscles burn calories and fat. The more muscle mass the greater the body's ability to burn calories and fat, even when not exercising. Rarely does exercise alone lead to weight loss. It also requires reducing calories and in Carol's case reducing carbohydrates as well.

Most diets don't work in the long run in that the body's metabolism slows down over a period of time when calories are sharply reduced. The body's defense against starvation is to store and conserve fat. Slowing metabolism results when calories are severely restricted. Calorie restriction diets may result in temporary weight loss. However, people typically regain most if not all of the weight lost due to calorie reduction. The key to permanent weight loss is to change both the nature and amount of calories consumed, yet without feeling deprived. For Carol and me, the how was a change to more vegetables, fruit, protein, virtual elimination of carbohydrates, and reduced sugar which meant no or limited desserts.

Specifically, the how for us involves a variety of fresh vegetables which we use for dipping into hummus; no or restricted carbohydrates; a variety of fresh fruit; beef, chicken or fish and limited desserts. Dessert typically is fresh pineapple spears. We allow ourselves the privilege of one piece of chocolate candy a day for each of us. If we get hungry between meals we have a couple of spoons of pomegranate seeds. This has resulted in weight loss for both of us.

We started the weight loss diet on January 30, 2014. At that point Carol weighed 190 pounds. As of December 15, 2014, she weighed 152 pounds for a total weight loss of 38 pounds. My weight has dropped from 165 to 158 pounds. I now weigh 10 pounds less than my senior year in high school when I played football at 168 pounds. Losing weight as a couple is advantageous over trying to lose weight individually.

Carol's weight loss has been noticed by other Y members. On March 2, 2014, one of the women at the Y said, "You've lost weight." Other people have said, "You look as skinny as a pencil," and "You are glowing," and other frequent compliments on how good she looks from Y members and friends from church. This reinforces her motivation.

One of the added benefits in losing weight for Carol has been going through her clothes closet and finding smaller clothes which she has not worn in a long time. She is like a kid in a candy shop. This is like shopping for clothes without spending any money. This will continue as she continues to lose weight. She feels increasingly more attractive in her clothes as she continues to lose weight. I also love it and support it, of course.

We are very happy with this turn of events. Can our results be replicated? Of course we cannot say that anyone else who follows our journey will experience the same improvement in vision, smell and sexuality. On the other hand improvement in libido cannot be ruled out since everyone's MS course is different. More needs to be learned.

Carol continues to see progress in multiple ways. This is noticed by many people. Most of the time she is the only one using a walker at the Y which makes her very visible when we work out together on the fitness center floor. When we work out at the Y, people comment on her improvement. She is often told by others at the Y that she is an inspiration to them. When we meet someone that she has not seen for some time, they comment on how good she looks. When she went to get a haircut, the owner of the shop who hadn't seen her in several months volunteered that she looked wonderful. One of her buddies in the exercise class told her that she could see improvement in her posture. On a later visit with Dr. Zhou, he sat down in front of her and without further examination, asked in exclamation, "What are you doing?" We told him again that she was doing ST. Her gains are noticeable to others.

Carol's quality of life is so much better than before we started on this journey. As a result, my stress is less and my quality of life is better, too. The sex is good and life is good.

## Chapter 3: What You May Do

What then might anyone with MS do to take control and improve the quality of his or her life? Remember, an important assumption is that patients are in charge of their illness. If you have MS, you are in charge of your illness and this is done in collaboration with your doctor and your caregiver(s). The above details Carol's and my journey to reverse disability with ST and thus improve our overall quality of life. Of course, we cannot promise the same results. On the other hand, you may find it is worth the effort. Following is what you can do.

## ST and Primary Progressive MS

I suggest that others with MS may be able to do what Carol and I have done as described previously. People with primary progressive multiple sclerosis (PPMS) are often told by their doctors that there are no disease modifying drugs for this form of MS. Further, they are often told there is nothing medically that can be done for them. That is a disheartening message. PPMS does not present with relapses followed by periods of remission. Rather, PPMS presents the patients with slow but relentless progression of the disease with increasing disability in multiple areas.

I realize that ST is not a cure for MS. Nor is there any cure for MS. On the other hand, what would happen if someone with PPMS was on an aggressive program of ST and flexibility exercises as described above? Would there be at least the possibility of slowing the progression of disability? I have reviewed many studies on ST and MS and have not found any studies that explore ST and progressive MS.

Peggy Min is a dear friend who has PPMS. She attends Trinity Presbyterian Church in Nashville with Carol and me. She and her mother were both diagnosed with PPMS about the same time. Her mother eventually died from complications due to her disease. Peggy is quadriplegic due to MS. She lives in an apartment with support from a team that provides 24 hour a day caregiving. She is able to speak, eat and can move her wheel chair with her chin or is pushed by a caregiver. She has a voice activated computer which she uses effectively.

Peggy is very active and goes to church on a regular basis. Beyond that, she is an active volunteer with me with a group of inmates on death row at Riverbend Maximum Security Institution in Nashville. Together, we lead a bible study group there once a week. She is an inspiration to inmates and guards alike. She also participates in Christmas caroling on death row during the holiday season.

A documentary film was made of Peggy by Demetria Kalodimos who is the evening news anchor on WSMV, the local NBC affiliate, with me as a producer. Demetria was the Executive Producer, Director and Editor. The five minute short appeared on the Neuro Film Festival and can be viewed on You Tube. It can be seen by searching for, *"Fearless: Peggy Min Faces MS."*

Peggy believes very strongly that if she had had followed an aggressive course of ST then her disability would have taken a slower course. This is anecdotal and can't be verified. It does need to be the subject of an observational research study.

Beyond that, there is nothing to prevent someone with PPMS from embarking on their own ST program. This is especially true when people with PPMS are routinely told by neurologists that there is nothing that can be done for them. Remember, the patient is responsible for his or her illness.

For someone who is newly diagnosed with relapsing MS, when there may just be the beginning of symptoms but without much disability walking, it is wise to start ST early after diagnosis. After all, there has been ample evidence already cited that ST needs to be a part of one's exercise routine throughout life even in the absence of a chronic disease. It is even more important to start ST in the early stages of disability when the range of disability is minimal, 2.0 to moderate 3.0 on EDSS. If the disability has progressed to 4.0, relatively severe disability, to 6.0, assistance required to walk, then it is even more essential to start aggressive ST to prevent further disability on the one hand or even reverse disability as we discovered with Carol.

Gym membership is very desirable. This provides a wide range of free weights and resistance machines as well as other amenities. For those sixty-five and older, the Silver Sneakers Program which is available through some Medicare Advantage Plans provides free membership to the YMCA and other privately owned fitness centers. Medicare Advantage plans are available to those who are enrolled in Medicare Parts A and B. Our Medicare

Advantage plan has no premium. The only premium we pay is for Part B of Medicare.

If gym membership is not an option due to membership costs or other factors then for a modest investment simple home equipment may be purchased. A basic set of equipment includes dumbbells, with a pair of 3, 5, 8, 10, 12 and 15 pounds or more of weight. Therabands or Resistance tubes can provide a variety of resistance exercises. The Magic Circle exercise ring also known as a Pilates Ring may be used to strengthen the inner thighs or a variety of other resistance exercises. Stability balls may be purchased if such can be used without risk of falling. Beyond that, a chair or bench is needed for seated exercises. Something as simple as walking up stairs will strengthen the quadriceps and *Ileus Soleus*. Floor mats make floor exercises more comfortable.

Body-weight squats may be done routinely at home. Doing squats from a seated position gives greater stability if maintaining balance is a problem. "Squats are absolutely incredible. They build full body strength as you use your core to stabilize and keep everything aligned. The glutes and hamstrings are very large muscles so buy (sic) utilizing them you tend to burn a lot of fat. Squats invigorate your nervous system and help your stress response since the squat is a naturally defensive position. They can even help your digestion and the regularity of your bowel movements. This is essentially the swiss (sic) army knife of exercise. ... First off, if you can set a goal of trying to complete 100 squats each day you will see a noticeable change in your body in just a matter of weeks.[43]

---

[43] Meisel, Ari, "Squats: The Absolutely Incredible Secret to Staying in Shape," *TheDaily Beast,* 1/2/14

"Squats: The Absolutely Incredible Secret to Staying in Shape"[44]

The 100 squats do not have to be done in one set but may be spaced out over the course of a day. The 100 squats number is a standard for someone without MS. With MS, the number of squats may need to be less. If you

---

[44] *Ibid*

can do the squats with stability and no risk of falling, you may hold dumbbells in each hand or wear weights around your waist to increase resistance and create more muscle mass.

Calf muscles may be strengthened by standing on a two-by-four on the balls of the feet and performing calf raises. If it can be done safely then holding dumbbells in each hand or using a weight belt increases the weight lifted. Modified push-ups may be done from a kneeling position if full-body extension push-ups are not possible. Or modify the push-ups by pushing against a wall.

A significant benefit would be for the caregiver and the person with MS to work out together. I do my own workout between Carol's set of reps on each exercise. This allows for her to rest between sets while I do my sets.

This joint work-out accrues benefits to our marriage. We consider our workouts a "date." I keep myself in shape while helping Carol by spotting her with free weights, and placing weights on the resistance machines. If a person with MS and caregiver work out together, both may be expected to benefit both physically and mentally. If our program is followed then we would expect similar results with either a slowing or reversal of disability if the exercise is done at our level of intensity and frequency. In addition both caregiver and the person with MS should experience a decrease in stress because the activities of daily living are more manageable.

Those with MS who do not have a caregiver will need to work out a ST plan on their own along the lines outlined above. Virtually all of the people I see in the fitness center at the YMCA are there as individuals. There are some couples besides Carol and me. One of those couples is a husband with his wife who has MS. We see a spike in attendance at the Y after January 1st and then attendance levels off and we see the regulars throughout the year. Motivation to change does not come through a New Year's resolution.

For someone with MS, the commitment to change comes from the desire to live a healthier and happier lifestyle. For someone with MS, the lifestyle will be healthier and happier if the symptoms of MS can be slowed on the one hand or reversed on the other.

It is said, "Insanity is doing the same thing over and over again and expecting different results." For those whose MS has led to more disability, it is all the more incumbent upon them to change future outcomes for the better. ST as described here is that way. Another saying I like is, "If what you're doing is not working, try something different." If what you are doing has not slowed or reversed your disability, try something different. Try ST for a minimum of six months and see what happens.

### For Neurologists and Other Medical Care Providers

I've heard some neurologists say they don't have the time to spend with patients to tell them about the importance of exercise and in particular ST. I heard one neurologist with a large MS practice in Knoxville tell the MS support group we attended that with ST, "You have to be careful you don't become 'muscle bound.'"

Heather Henke has MS and she and Carol are good friends. Heather has embarked on an aggressive conditioning program with a personal trainer. Carter Hayes has trained people who made the finals of *The Biggest Loser* on television. Her regimen with him includes ST. She also has a gluten-free diet. She has had remarkable results.

She was told by her neurologist, a well-known researcher in MS at Vanderbilt University, "Enjoy the gains while you can." This statement assumes the gains will not last. I am greatly disturbed by these assertions by well-known and highly regarded neurologists.

I assume that most neurologists are interested in what the best course of treatment for their patients should be. I assume they would like to slow the progression of disability and loss of function or even bring it to a halt with their patients. Let me respond to the above assertions.

As to not having enough time to tell their MS patients about the *necessity* of ST in managing their MS, the neurologists don't have to spend their time with the patient doing this. That could be done in thirty seconds by the doctor. The details may be assigned to the office nurse. It still comes with the authority of the doctor. When a doctor tells patients they need to do ST for their MS it carries greater weight than if a person who is not a physician says it. The office practice should have physical handouts on the benefits of exercise and in particular ST benefits for MS. They should also have a list of MS support groups. The nurse can tell patients these things.

There are some patients who will not take disease modifying drugs. It is even more important to share this information with them. This is with the understanding that many patients will not act on this information. But some will. Remember, patients are responsible for their illness. Having said that, the patient cannot take action if the information is not given and strongly emphasized.

The assertion that, "You have to be careful you don't become 'muscle bound,'" is an old expression but "muscle bound" is not well-defined and is factually inaccurate. I was taken off guard by the statement and said, "Women don't become muscle bound." I was too surprised to respond further.

The concept of muscle bound is a dated concept. It was used in some athletic circles including major league baseball to debunk weight training. It apparently had to do with the mistaken belief that weight training would lead to a loss of flexibility. This is simply not true. In modern athletic training, elite athletes in virtually every sport use a combination of ST and flexibility training at all levels from high school through the highest levels of professional sports. Major League baseball players, NFL football players, NBA players, track and field athletes, gymnasts and Olympic swimmers use ST and flexibility training routinely. When Michael Phelps, Olympic gold medalist in swimming, is not in the pool he is training in the weight room. The goal for someone with MS is not to become an elite athlete. The goal is to slow or reverse disability and improve one's quality of life.

To tell a MS patient who has shown gains physically and mentally in her exercise program including ST and through diet to, "Enjoy it while you can," assumes disability will progress regardless of what she does. If believed by the patient, it becomes self-limiting. This is a self-fulfilling prophecy. A self-fulfilling prophecy becomes true because the person believing in it acts as if it were true and so it becomes true. This is more likely to be the case if the person making the statement is a well-regarded expert in the field of MS research. However, the statement is not supported by evidence-based research, particularly research in the area of aggressive ST and MS.

Carol and I attend numerous MS support groups. At one of the support groups we attended, the MS support nurse *who* led a discussion on managing MS symptoms said, "MS disability cannot be reversed." This is another example of a trusted authority on MS making a self-fulfilling prophecy to a room full of MS patients and caregivers. I politely told her privately as we were leaving that we had reversed Carol's disability through aggressive ST. We have found the statement of the MS nurse oft repeated but it is not supported by our experience nor by evidence-based research.

It should be noted that for decades there was a common belief that people with MS should not exercise. Since then, that mistaken belief has been debunked. "The Society is not only interested in research into potential drug treatment, but also lifestyle and alternative/complementary treatments and we fund more research in this area than any other MS organization in the world. For example studies funded by the Society played a pivotal role in reversing the mistaken belief that exercise was not a good idea for people with MS."[45] I suggest that it is a mistaken belief that MS disability cannot be reversed. I suggest that more evidence based research is needed in this area.

Carol and I have often been told by well-meaning people not to overdo it, meaning her ST. She was even told that by Carter Hayes. We didn't listen. The body is a marvelous feedback system. In the normal course of MS, her fatigue levels vary greatly. When her energy is low, we limit the intensity or length of the workout. But over the long haul, we continue to be aggressive and push even higher weights as she continues to make progress.

---

[45] Rosenblat, Arney, Associate Vice President, Public Affairs, "Response to a Dear Colleague letter asking about Society dollars at work," National MS Society, September 1, 2010.

There is plenty of research on the benefits of ST with MS. However, the studies I've found were typically limited to moderate resistance exercises focused on the legs, lower back and abdomen for as little as 30 minutes twice a week. "Researchers reported improvements in muscle strength and function, and reductions in self-reported fatigue among eight patients participating in a two-month study evaluating resistance training. ... Training included moderate, supervised resistance exercises focused on the legs, lower back and abdomen for 30 minutes twice each week. At the end of eight weeks, the patients had significantly stronger muscles of the leg, were able to walk better and reported significantly less fatigue and disability."[46] Other studies reported similar results.[47] Another significant study found that, "...it is known that the first neuromuscular adaptations to strength training are more neural than muscular. Positive neural changes are especially important in a population afflicted with a neurological disorder. Neural recruitment gained through physical activity may have a favorable functional outcome, although this may be limited by the severity the MS lesions already present. This suggests that resistance training may be an early intervention strategy in persons with MS that may help to maintain function and hopefully, limit exacerbation of MS symptoms. In fact, in all research

---

[46] Boyles, Salynn, "Pumping Iron Helps Strengthen MS Patients Study Shows Improvements in Muscle Strength, Fatigue, Disability," WebMd Health News, Jan. 19, 2005, ©2005 WebMd., Inc. All rights reserved.
[47] "Effects of resistance training in multiple sclerosis," Abstract, International Journal of Sports Medicine, 2009 April 30 (4): 24550. Epub 2009 Feb 6.

previously mentioned concerning strength training in individuals with MS, no MS related exacerbations were reported and there were no reports of increased MS related symptoms...."[48]

Dr. Samuel Hunter, M.D., is an internationally well-known MS expert and researcher in MS who practices an integrative approach to MS in Franklin. In private conversations with him he has indicated that ST creates changes that are as much neural as muscular.

This link between exercise or physical inactivity and changes in the brain are noted in another article. "A number of studies have shown that exercise can remodel

---

[48] Gutierrez, Gregory Michael, 'EFFECTS OF AN EIGHT-WEEK PROGRESSIVE RESISTANCE TRAINING PROGRAM ON BALANCE IN PERSNS WITH MULTIPLE SCLEROSIS, A Thesis Presented to the Graduate School of the University of Florida in Partial Fulfillment of the Requirements for the Degree of Master of Science, University of Florida, 2005, Copyright 2005 by Gregory Michael Gutierrez, p. 28

the brain by prompting the creations of new brain cells and inducing other changes. Now it appears that inactivity, too, can remodel the brain, …" [49] Is it possible these improvements in Carol's vision, smell and sexuality as noted earlier have occurred due to her aggressive ST and flexibility exercises? This cannot be ruled out.

Having said this, I have not found any studies on aggressive resistance training on muscles from neck to feet coupled with flexibility exercises from neck to feet. I have not found any studies of aggressive ST an hour in duration and five days a week in frequency.

Carol has reversed disability in multiple ways. Our anecdotal experience suggests that this be explored with research studies. Our experience suggests that well

---

[49] Reynolds, Gretchen, "This Is Your Brain on the Couch," *The New York Times,* the *Science Times,* January 28, 2014, p. D4

founded research is needed on aggressive ST for MS patients as described here. I will lend my support and what we have learned as an advisor to any MS researcher who may be interested in developing a rigorous study.

## Chapter 4: In Summary

If Carol can do what we have described in reversing her MS disability I suggest others may do it as well. Slowing loss of function is also a laudable goal. The Nike slogan is, "Just do it." You can have excuses or you can slow and maybe reverse disability and restore function but you can't have both. Maybe you have resolved to make a positive change in your life only to find you didn't do what you said you would do. So it is with New Year's resolutions.

There are common excuses we make to not do something which would be good for us. A common excuse is, "I don't have the time." That statement is not about how much time you have. Everyone has the same amount of time in a given week. What the "I don't have time" excuse is saying is that something is just not as important as other things. It is saying that the time spent on ST exercise is just not a priority compared to other things.

How much time is needed for aggressive ST and flexibility exercises? Carol and I work out two hours a day Sunday through Wednesday and flexibility and Pilates exercises on Friday for one hour. This is a total of 9 hours a week. In addition she works out for a half hour on Tuesday and Thursday morning with the group led by Carter Hayes as a personal trainer. This is a total of 9 hours a week. We factor in 15 minutes of rest for her between ST and flexibility and Pilates. And 30 minutes round trip for travel to and from the Y. This is a total of about 10 hours a week. Given our results it has been worth it to us. You can have excuses or you can slow or reverse disability but you can't have both.

Another excuse is "I don't think it will work," or "I don't think it will work for me." Really? And how did you arrive at the conclusion something will work or not for you unless you do it *as prescribed* for an extended period of time? The experience with our program was that she experienced positive results within a week. Over two years the results have been even more dramatic.

It may be that some who have read this will conclude it takes too much time or is too difficult. If that is the case then something is better than nothing. You may cut down the length and frequency of ST workouts and still have some gains at preventing further disability. Cited above, even a thirty minute workout of moderate intensity two times a week may produce positive results.

One problem for some with MS may be the negative statements of people who may discredit and belittle efforts to change life for the better. These people may be well-intentioned but misinformed, some with impressive credentials. Other people who discredit or belittle one's efforts to change may be people they love or who love them. It is important to take charge of your life. No one else around you lives in your body and experiences your MS as you do. You are the ultimate judge of your thoughts, feelings and behavior and not anyone else. If your caregiver can't or won't workout with you, then work out on your own. Feel free to ask gym employees or others who are working out to help you as needed. "Just do it."

## Addendum

The following are instructions for using ST and resistance training exercises to help improve strength, endurance and overall quality of life for those with MS.

This is the regimen that Carol and I have developed.

TECHNIQUE

- Drink ice water. Hydration is essential but ice water will cool the core to keep from becoming overheated.

- Begin with lower weights and over time move up to heavier weights. This will decrease the possibility of muscle soreness at the beginning. As weight is increased, reps will decrease quite naturally.

- Generally do three sets of each exercise. To begin, do 15 reps and as weight is increased the reps may be reduced to as few as 5 per set. If particularly fatigued, do fewer sets.

- During the exertion phase of the rep, push to full extension and do not bring the weight to full rest. Keep continual pressure on during the rep.

- As reps increase there will be a decrease in range of motion, indicating muscle failure as you tire. Keep doing the exercise to almost full failure when you can't lift the weight anymore.
- Breathe out over the lips during exertion and breathe in through the nose while lowering the weight.

EXERCISE REGIMEN

- Schedule: Work outs 4 to 6 times a week. At six times a week take one day off for rest. At 4 times a week, take a day off (or two) between sessions. Or, as described above if you do not work out that often then reduce the frequency to 3 times a week

- Core Exercises. Do the core each time you exercise. The core is important in that the abdomen and lower back are important in getting off the ground or floor in the event of a fall. Also, with a tighter core you will look better in clothes. With the Lower Back Extension Machine do up to 30 reps. With the Abdominal Crunch Machine do up to 30 reps. Core strength is needed for balance.
- Legs: Work all leg systems every other workout. These are the lifting muscles needed for walking, endurance in walking and balance.
    1) Seated Leg Press machine: Works buttocks and quadriceps. Do three sets increasing the weight and decreasing reps over time until reaching a maximum weight. Even

then, keep pushing the weight higher. (Use this formula unless noted otherwise.)

2) Seated Leg Curl Machine: Works hamstrings.

3) Seated Hip Abduction Machine: Works hips. The exertion phase moves the legs outward while seated.

4) Seated Hip Adduction (same as on the Seated Hip Abduction Machine). Works inside the thighs/groin. The exertion phase of exercise moves the legs inward.

5) Standing Calf Raises: On Calf Raise machine

6) Thigh Lift: Leg Lift Machine: Grab the handles, back against the pad and with elbows on the elbow pads. Lift the thighs up as far as possible with the legs bent. If doing both legs at the same time is too difficult

then alternate between the legs. Do as many reps as possible up to 30 reps and three sets. Strengthens the *Ileus Soleus*.

- Arms: Work all arm systems every other workout. The arms are needed for upper body strength which is needed to get off the ground or floor in the event of a fall. This will also aid in strength of hands in gripping and aid in dexterity to fingers.

1) Seated Press Machine (Vertical Press): Works deltoids and triceps. Alternate with Chest Press Machine. This works pectorals and triceps.

2) Seated Lat Machine: Works Latissimus Dorsi (lats) and Biceps.

3) Lateral Raise Machine: Works Deltoids and Trapeziums.

4) Seated Concentration Biceps Curls: With a dumbbell in one hand, place your elbow in the inner part of thigh then lift the dumbbell with full extension to chin. Alternate to other hand and thigh. Works the Biceps.

- Allow 15-20 minutes of rest between ST and Stretching, Balance and Pilates exercises.

## BALANCE AND STRETCHING

- For balance, stand on one foot with left arm and right leg extended forward. Hold for 30 seconds. Alternate to right arm and left leg extended forward. If unsteady, hold on to something with the free hand for stability. Carol holds on to her walker. (Hold for 30 seconds on all the following exercises.)

- Lying on back on workout mat with left leg extended on floor, toes up, pull right knee to chest. Alternate to right leg extended on floor, toes up, pull left knee to chest. Stretches buttocks and groin.

- Lying Knee-to Chest Stretch: Lying on your back, keep one leg flat on the mat. Use your hands to bring the other knee to your chest.

- In seated position on mat, reach between legs and move further inn 5 second increments. Then move to same stretch with nose over left knee for 10 seconds and then to nose over right knee for 10 seconds. Stretches hamstrings.

- Lying on the floor on mat with the right leg bent toward chest and left leg flat on the floor, pull right leg to the left. Alternate with the left leg bent toward chest and right leg flat on the floor and pull left leg over to the right. Stretches the hip flexor.

- Kegel Exercises: Lying on the floor on mat, do 30 contractions each of anal sphincter and bladder sphincter. This strengthens those smooth muscles and improves bladder and bowel control. (The number of episodes of loss of bladder or bowel control for Carol has been reduced to near zero. This was the pivotal part of control along with Detrol, a stool softener twice a day, Metamucil and two fingers high of prune juice, all on a daily basis.)

- Ankle Strengthening: With your workout partner, lay on back on mat. Have your workout partner press with his/her hands against your feet as you move them inward against his/her isometric pressure for 40 seconds. Do 3 sets. Repeat pushing up with the toes of the feet against the isometric pressure. Repeat with isometric pressure as you move the toes of feet outward. Repeat with pressing the feet against your partner's thighs who is in a kneeling position. This strengthens the ankles in all four directions. It may be expected to reduce or eliminate foot drop as it has done with Carol.

PILATES – Strengthen the Core. All are on a mat unless noted otherwise.

- Planks: Lying on mat on floor on your abdomen place your elbows on the mat directly perpendicular to your shoulders. Lift you abdomen off the mat for as long as you are able. Do 3 sets. Increase the lengths of time you can hold the position. Strengthens the lower back. Posture should improve.
- Pilates Darts: This is a back strengthening exercise. Lie on our stomach on the mat with

legs together. And arms at your sides. Place your hands behind your neck and lift your upper body/chest slightly off the mat. Keep your abdominal muscles pulled in. Your head is an extension of your spine. Your gaze will be down. Hold for an inhale and exhale to lengthen and lower your body to the floor. This strengthens the lower back muscles and will improve posture. It is also recommended for people with lower back pain.

- Inner Thigh Press: Lay on your back with your knees bent and your feet hip distance apart. Place a yoga block or squishy ball between your knees just above the bone. Inhale. Exhale as you squeeze your abdominals and squeeze the circle. Hold for 3 counts. Inhale to gently release the circle. Repeat 8 times. Do 2 sets of 8 if you are able.

- Toe Taps: Laying on your back, lift one leg at a time into the tabletop position (shin parallel to floor). Keeping the leg position of bent knee, tap the toes of the foot (or heel) down onto the mat and then left it back up again. Do not let the back arch on this. Do all you can to maintain your pelvic position and a stable spine. Repeat on the other leg in the table top position. Repeat 8 times for both legs.

- Deltoid Lifts: Sit up straight with your arms low and in front of you with wrists crossed. Make fists with your hands. Inhale to prepare, exhale to lift the elbows up to shoulder height while bending the elbows. Gently release to the starting position on an inhalation and begin again. Repeat 8 times.

- Wall Roll Down: In a standing position with your feet about 12 inches from the wall and back against the wall, reach forward with your arms extended so that you back is extended with just your butt touching the wall. Do wall roll down 5 times. Should help improve standing and balance.

**STANDING STRETCHING EXERCISES**

- Neck Stretch: In a standing position, bring your right arm behind you and grab it with your left hand. Tilt your head to the left as you pull gently with your left hand. Repeat on the other side.

- Head Retraction: Put hands lightly on back of head. Pinch should blades together as you push your head back.

- Triceps Stretch: Stand with your hand behind your neck and your elbow pointing upwards. Then use your other hand (or a rope or towel) to pull your elbow down. If you cannot do that, then have your workout partner stretch your triceps for you. Repeat with other triceps.

- Stork Position - Also known as Standing Quadriceps Pull: Stand tall with abs engaged, feet together, with arms by sides. Bring right heel toward butt and grasp top of foot with right hand. Extend left arm overhead (or place on a chair or rail to help balance. Press right foot into hand to increase stretch along the front of thigh bringing your heel to your butt. Repeat on left side. If this is too difficult, have your workout partner lift your feet so your heels touch your butt.

- Leaning Heel Back Call Stretch: Stand upright and lean against a wall. Place one foot as far from the wall as is comfortable and make sure that your toes are facing forward and your heel is on the ground. Repeat with the opposite leg. Or, keep your back leg straight and lean toward the wall. Stand on a stair step with the ball of the foot on the edge of the step and drop the heel to stretch the hamstring and then alternate to the other foot. Stretches the calves and hamstrings.

- Stork Position. With left arm extended horizontally, curl right leg back and pull leg with right hand on right foot at the toes until the heel touches the right buttock. Alternate with right arm extended and curl left leg back as before until heel touches left buttock. Stretches the quadriceps. (If you cannot reach your feet with your hand then loop a rope or resistance tube over your foot and pull up your foot over your shoulder to stretch the quads.  Or have a caregiver or workout partner stretch you.)

"He gives power to the faint, and to him who has no might he increases strength.  Even youths shall faint and be weary, and young men shall fall exhausted; but _they who wait for the Lord shall renew their strength_, they shall mount up with wings like eagles, they shall run and not be weary, they shall walk and not faint." Isaiah 40: 29-31

If anyone wishes further information regarding this book, feel free to contact me as follows: David Phillipy dphillipy@comcast.net and (615) 554-5876 (Cell).

Made in the USA
Lexington, KY
17 May 2015